TATTERSHALL CASTLE

Lincolnshire

THE NATIONAL TRUST

TATTERSHALL CASTLE is 3½ miles south-east of Woodhall Spa, off the A153 Sleaford to Louth road.

Acknowledgements

This guidebook has been written by Tracey Avery, formerly the Trust's Historic Buildings Representative responsible for Tattershall, drawing on the previous edition by Dr M. W. Thomson. Thanks are also due to Dr Michael Jones of Nottingham University for his comments on the text, to Dr John Martin Robinson for help with the heraldry, and to Mr P. Dixon for revising the plans of the castle from the originals drawn by W. Weir and F. G. Read.

Oliver Garnett

Photographs: Country Life Picture Library/Paul Barker pp. 4, 11, 12, 14, 15, 17, 19, 22, 23, 25 (top left), 30; Eton College/Courtauld Institute p. 26; Dick Makin Photography pp. 25 (bottom right), 27; National Trust pp. 13, 21, 28, 29, 32; National Trust Photographic Library/John Bethell pp. 5, back cover; NTPL/Andrew Butler front cover; NTPL/Neil Campbell-Sharp p. 18; NTPL/Brian Lawrence pp. 1, 9; NTPL/Mike Williams p. 6.

First published in Great Britain in 1997 by the National Trust
© 1997 The National Trust
Registered charity no. 205846

ISBN 978-1-84359-119-1

Reprinted with corrections 2002, 2004; reprinted 2005, 2007, 2009

Designed by James Shurmer

Phototypeset in Monotype Bembo Series 270 by Printessential Ltd, Smallfield, Surrey (15347)

Printed by Hawthornes for National Trust (Enterprises) Ltd, Heelis, Kemble Drive, Swindon, Wilts SN2 2NA on Cocoon Silk made from 100% recycled paper

CONTENTS

The Great Tower and the church of the Holy Trinity were both commissioned by Ralph Cromwell in the mid-fifteenth century

TATTERSHALL CASTLE

The Great Tower of Tattershall Castle still stands proud in the flat fen landscape of east Lincolnshire. One imagines the castle as an outpost, a purely defensive structure and so an uncomfortable place to live. Yet although today the castle appears solitary, the Great Tower once lay at the heart of a complex arrangement of buildings, walls and bridges, whose remains give us a rare picture of a large noble household in the later Middle Ages.

The first castle on this site was built in stone by Robert de Tateshale in the early thirteenth century; King John had granted his father a charter in 1201 to hold a weekly market in the village, in exchange for a trained goshawk. The younger de Tateshale, who had fought alongside Henry III in France, received a licence in 1231 to build a fortified stone house. It probably occupied the area within the inner moat and consisted of lengths of wall with round towers at each corner. Very little of this first castle can now be seen, but its layout determined the shape of what does still survive.

By the early fifteenth century Tattershall Castle had passed to Ralph, 3rd Baron Cromwell (1393–1456). In 1433 he was appointed Lord Treasurer to Henry VI (the medieval equivalent of Chancellor of the Exchequer), and he immediately began using the rewards of his high office to enlarge the castle. He built the 33.5-metres-high Great Tower, which is one of the masterpieces of medieval brickwork, vying in scale with the great cathedrals of that age. Its vast size was the most graphic statement possible of Cromwell's power. The magnificent chimneypieces in the main rooms proudly display his badge of office, the Treasurer's purse, and the coats of arms of the wealthy families with which the Cromwells had allied themselves by marriage. Tattershall was meant not only as a status symbol, but also to provide comfortable, well-lit accommodation for Cromwell and his guests: hence the large and elegant traceried windows, which could hardly have withstood a siege.

Tattershall was later owned by Kings of England from Edward IV to Henry VIII. During the sixteenth and seventeenth centuries the Earls of Lincoln occupied the castle, until 1693, when it was abandoned as a residence, and gradually decayed into a picturesque ruin.

In 1910 the chimneypieces were ripped out and sold, and the Great Tower faced the imminent threat of being demolished. Lord Curzon came to the rescue the following year, buying the site, excavating the moats and carefully restoring the buildings and reinstating the original chimneypieces. That Tattershall survives at all is a testimony to his campaign for the preservation of Britain's ancient monuments. The property was bequeathed to the National Trust on his death in 1925.

The chimneypiece on the third floor bears the treasurer's purse, the symbol of Cromwell's office and the source of this wealth and power. The arch at the bottom is carved with the Common Gromwell – a pun on Cromwell's name

TOUR OF THE CASTLE

THE WARDS

The castle grounds are roughly square in shape, bounded by an outer moat which encloses the Outer and Middle Wards and is fed by the River Bain. Another squarish moat in the middle surrounds the Inner Ward. The inner moat was the single enclosure for the thirteenth-century castle, while the outer moat was added by Lord Cromwell in the 1430s. The layout of the castle at this period can be visualised from the modern reconstruction illustrated on p. 7.

In Lord Cromwell's time, visitors to the castle would have first crossed the outer moat to the Outer Ward at a point north of the Great Tower near the present main road. Having stabled their horses, they would have crossed to the Middle Ward by another bridge which was defended by a gatehouse, fragments of which have survived. To penetrate the walled Inner Ward, on which the Great Tower stands, they would next have had to pass over a third bridge and possibly through a further gatehouse (now gone) before being admitted to the tower itself. This elaborate succession of bridges, moats and gatehouses was designed to foil attackers, as the whole route was commanded from the Inner Ward.

THE MIDDLE WARD

Today visitors enter the castle from the east, crossing a modern bridge directly on to the Middle Ward. In Lord Cromwell's day, this open space would have been covered in buildings. The only one to survive largely intact is the fifteenth-century 'guardhouse' on the left, which now houses an exhibition devoted to the history of the castle and some of the numerous images of the castle in its years as a picturesque ruin. It also contains the National Trust shop.

To the right of the path are the fragmentary remains of an unfinished brick range, which may have been lodgings for Lord Cromwell's retinue. Next to the bridge to the Outer Ward are the foundations of a small gatehouse with a doorway on the side nearest the moat. This modern bridge rests on fifteenth-century abutments.

Tattershall from the east in 1726; engraving after Samuel Buck

Reconstruction of Tattershall in Ralph Cromwell's time, when the Great Tower was surrounded by ranges of service buildings and protected by walls and gatehouses as well as moats

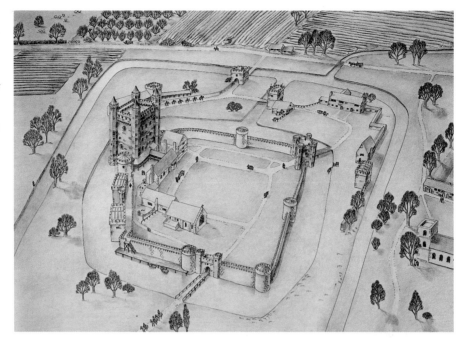

(Below) Plan of the Castle and Grounds

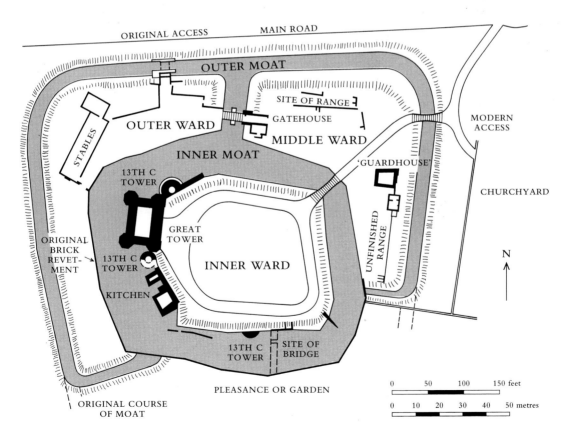

For the sake of clarity, the Outer Ward is described next, although it is more conveniently seen after the Inner Ward and the Great Tower.

THE OUTER WARD

The footings of the original entrance bridge can be seen on the right, towards the main road. The derelict two-storeyed brick building dominating the Outer Ward may have included stables on the ground floor and living quarters above. The south gable wall contained fireplaces at both levels; this end may have been partitioned off for minor officers.

The west façade of the Great Tower, its main display front, is best viewed from the Outer Ward. The large windows and free use of lozenge patterns in the brickwork both suggest that the Great Tower was intended primarily as an elegant residence rather than as a fortress.

THE INNER WARD

Visitors cross to the castle's Inner Ward over a modern bridge, which rests on fifteenth-century abutments. The projection in the moat on the outer side is the base of the former stone abutment for the thirteenth-century drawbridge encased in brick. In the engraving of 1726 by Samuel Buck (illustrated on p. 6) the front half of a gatehouse with corner turrets and portcullis is shown at the inner end of the bridge.

At the base of the Great Tower lay a range of buildings based around the earlier hall. Buck's view is distorted in scale and perspective, but we can infer from it that this hall was in front of and parallel to the tower. It had traceried windows and an oriel window on the right, terminating in a seventeenth-century cross-range. At right angles lay what was evidently the kitchen, while projecting still further into the courtyard were the remains of a chapel, with a fifteenth-century chantry chapel on its north side. Some remains of these earlier buildings can still be seen. Either side of the brick tower are the bases of the smaller towers which punctuated the walls enclosing Robert de Tateshale's earlier stone castle. The base on the north-east corner is better preserved, retaining part of its cylindrical shape on the inside and chamfered plinth on the outside.

Beyond the remains of the southern stone tower are brick foundations marking the site of the fifteenth-century kitchens, built to serve the new hall in the Great Tower. The larger foundations contain a circular well. The kitchens seem to have been kept busy, as the building accounts for 1472 record payments to William Horner, tiler, for 'repairing the kitchen chimneys [and] the oven hearth in the bakehouse' – probably only 30 to 40 years after they had been built.

A third thirteenth-century tower base is partly visible on the southern side of the Inner Ward. Beyond, the base of a pier is visible in the moat, and the stone corbels opposite – on the original curtain wall – once supported a bridge to the garden. There are thought to have been walled gardens which were originally enclosed by the outer moat. Across the field the remains of fish-ponds have been found alongside the River Bain.

Stone slabs in the centre of the large lawn mark the position of the chapel foundations, discovered during Lord Curzon's restorations.

THE GREAT TOWER

The Great Tower is a masterpiece of early English brickwork, 33.5 metres high with six storeys, which succeeded in combining fashionable tracery windows and a decorative parapet with an overall image of strength, providing more comfortable living conditions than had previously been expected in a fortress. It was built by Ralph, Lord Cromwell about 1434–46 using Ancaster limestone and over a million bricks made locally by a Dutch craftsman named Baldwin.

The bricks are laid in English bond: alternate rows of end-on headers and lengthways stretchers. The diaper pattern is achieved by interspersing the red bricks with headers which have been given a bluish patina by being fired at a higher temperature. The bricks measure about 21cm long by 10cm deep by 5cm thick. Bricks only 4cm thick had previously been imported from Flanders, but by the fifteenth century the larger thickness had become standard.

The tower's façade is a good example of the transition from a defensive stronghold to one that gives the illusion of impenetrability. The parapets between the turrets contain real machicolations (openings between supporting corbels from which missiles could be dropped on attackers). However, the smaller machicolations around the turrets are

The east and north fronts of the Great Tower

purely ornamental. The large windows, mostly of two lights with traceried heads, start at the ground floor, and so could not have withstood attackers who managed to reach the Inner Ward.

Buck's view shows that each turret was once capped by a little spire formed by a lead-covered frame of wood with a crocketed finial. During Lord Curzon's restoration, dummy spires were erected, but they were not made a permanent feature.

THE EAST FRONT

In Cromwell's time, the ground floor of the Great Tower would have been partly hidden by the hall of the older castle, which has now disappeared. The curious flattening of the inner turrets was to allow

for passageways in the space between the tower and the hall. Rows of joist holes for the upper passage can still be seen on this façade between the ground and first floors. These passages were an integral part of the Great Tower, as they provided the only link between the basement and the ground floor, and between these levels and the three upper rooms. The tower was not designed as a self-sufficient building like a Norman keep, but to provide a set of grand apartments in which Cromwell could receive his most important visitors. The three doorways on the east front were originally part of the ground-floor passage. The left-hand one leads to the upper rooms, the central to the basement, and the right-hand to the ground-floor Parlour.

Just outside the right-hand door is the base of a spiral staircase which once led up to the first-floor passage, communicating in turn with a doorway on the staircase in the south-east turret. The object clearly was to allow direct access from the upper chambers of the tower to either the Parlour or the high table of the hall without having to approach at ground level.

The Interior

The layout of the building is extremely simple. The rooms are arranged in a vertical hierarchy, with the least important at the bottom and the most important and private at the top. The six storeys comprise a vaulted rectangular basement and four floors topped by a parapet level. Each level increases slightly in size, as well as in the quality of the decorative features, as they ascend and the walls become thinner. Three of the four octagonal corner turrets have brick-vaulted rooms at each level, which provided additional accommodation to rooms and passages built into the side walls, leaving just one great central room at each level, heated by a single large fireplace. The south-east corner contains the spiral staircase.

The vaulted corner turrets have survived intact, but the wooden floors of the large central rooms rotted and collapsed after the castle was abandoned in the late seventeenth century. During Lord Curzon's restoration these were replaced with lime ash floors – a common flooring material in the East Midlands. The main modern restorations comprise the floors, the roof, the window glass, the tracery in the ground-floor windows and the battlements and chimneys.

LATRINES

Shafts run from top to bottom in the thickness of the wall in the south-east and north-east corners of the building. They serviced the latrines at each floor level, discharging into sumps at the bottom, with outlets to the moat, and open at the top for ventilation. They are now used for draining rainwater from the roof.

The doors hanging in the central and left-hand doorways on the ground floor are ancient and, until recently, thought to be the only original woodwork in the Great Tower.

Go through the central door into the basement.

Basement

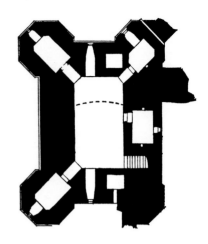

THE BASEMENT

The steps lead down to the basement, which is spanned by a fine brick vault of very low pitch. The floor is of brick, with a small well in the centre, its position marked by an area of floor tiles.

Although only lit by two small windows and the doorway, the basement was probably intended to be used as a servants' hall with storerooms. Torches and braziers may have provided additional light. The room within the thickness of the east wall contains two niches, which may have been aumbries (wall cupboards), and as the room once had a door which could have been locked, it may have been used as a larder for storing valuable provisions such as sugar and spices. The walls here are the thickest in the castle, at 4.25 metres. This room is said to have been used as a prison during the Civil War.

The south-west corner turret contains fragments of original roof beams.

Return up the steps and turn left. The right-hand door leads into the ground floor.

THE GROUND FLOOR

The Parlour

The principal room was probably intended as a parlour: the 'public' room for senior members of the household with smaller rooms where the business of the estate may have been carried out. The staff probably ate together in this room, with Lord Cromwell's family and guests dining on the floor

*The Parlour
chimneypiece*

above; this division of usage seems to mark the trend towards greater segregation in the late Middle Ages.

STAINED GLASS

The stained-glass panels in the windows depict the coats of arms of former owners of the castle and were designed by Clayton & Bell and made by Arthur Dix of H. G. Wright. They were commissioned in 1918 by Lord Curzon, whose own armorial bearings appear in the left-hand panel of the south window. The dates against each name indicate the period of ownership. The original cartoons for the windows can be seen in the museum.

The modern window in the north-west turret was commissioned in 1995 to celebrate the National Trust's Centenary. It was designed by Mr Ronald Whiting, following a competition in *Country Living* magazine, and made by Chapel Studios of Kings Langley.

CHIMNEYPIECE

The crenellated chimneypiece here is the finest of the four in the Great Tower, although it has suffered more damage than the others, because the ground floor was at one time used to hold cattle.

In the central spandrel is Cromwell's coat of arms, flanked by panels containing either the Treasurer's purse (a reference to Cromwell's position as Lord Treasurer) with his motto '*Nay je droit*' ('Have I not the right?'), or the coats of arms of Cromwell and the families into which his married.

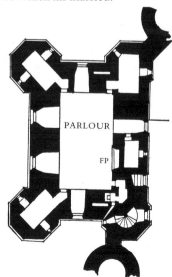

Ground Floor

11

TOP ROW, LEFT TO RIGHT:

1 *Ten annulets, four, three, two, one* (Vipont)

2, 4, 7, 9 *Treasurer's purse and motto* (Cromwell)

3 *A lion rampant* (Albini)

5 *Vaire a fess* (Marmion)

6 *Ermine a fess* (Bernack)

8 *A bend and chief* (Cromwell), *quartering a chequy a chief ermine* (Tateshale), *impaling a fess dancetty between ten billets* (Deyncourt)

10 *A bend and chief* (Cromwell), *quartering a chequy a chief ermine* (Tateshale)

BOTTOM ROW, LEFT TO RIGHT:

1, 3, 7, 9 *Treasurer's purse and motto* (Cromwell)

2 *Bendy of ten* (Clifton)

4 *A fess dancetty between ten billets* (Deyncourt)

5 (Central spandrel) *A bend and chief* (Cromwell)

6 *Two cinquefoils, a dexter canton* (Driby)

8 *Barry of six, a bend* (Grey of Rotherfield)

Earlier medieval fireplaces had a hood projecting out from the wall to prevent the smoke from coming back into the room, so the development of the chimney flue and stack allowing flush fireplaces was an innovative addition to Cromwell's tower.

LATRINE

In the south-east corner of the room a passage leads to a garderobe or latrine, ventilated by two shafts, one to the south wall and the other in the east wall, the outer opening of which is visible above the basement door.

EXHIBITION

There are display panels in the north-west turret of each floor of the castle showing how the rooms may have been used in the fifteenth century.

Leave by the entry door, turn right, and walk along the east front until you reach the far door in the south-east turret.

THE STAIRCASE

The newel staircase has stone treads of generous proportions and a finely carved, countersunk stone handrail. There are two doorways on the left of the staircase. The second (now blocked) must have

The spiral staircase in the south-east turret provides the only access to the upper floors

allowed access from the kitchens, through the earlier stone mural tower, to the hall on the first floor.

All three upper rooms have lobbies or chambers entered from the staircase, let into the thickness of the east wall and lit by their own windows.

THE FIRST FLOOR

The Great Hall

The central room has doorways leading to an entrance lobby next to the staircase and to a turret room at the further end. It is thought that this room was used as Lord Cromwell's Great Hall for entertaining guests. Also, it would have been easily accessible from the kitchens. Like the other two upper rooms, there are corbels high on the windowless wall at one end, transversely grooved above. These were intended to support a baldaquin or canopy hung over a high table. There are wooden blocks on the wall, either for a rail for hanging tapestries or for fixing wainscoting. The building accounts for 1434–5 include an item for '£7 for 200 boards called waynscott, provided by my lord [Cromwell] at Hull'. It is unlikely that any bare brickwork was left exposed; it would probably have been plastered above the wainscoting. The original ceilings would have been carved or painted.

CHIMNEYPIECE

The chimneypiece, again crenellated on supporting columns, bears roundels carved with Cromwell's Treasurer's purse and coat of arms, and those of his ancestors.

LEFT TO RIGHT:

1, 8 *Treasurer's purse and motto* (Cromwell)

2 *A chequy a chief ermine* (Tateshale)

First Floor

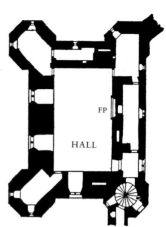

3 *St Michael slaying the Dragon*

4 *A bend and chief* (Cromwell), *quartering a chequy a chief ermine* (Tateshale), *impaling a fess dancetty between ten billets* (Deyncourt)

5 *A bend and chief* (Cromwell), *quartering a chequy a chief ermine* (Tateshale); *a helmet; supporters, two woodmen* (Cromwell)

The Great Hall chimneypiece in 1912

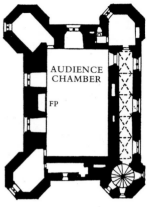

Second Floor

(Right)
The Audience Chamber

The vaulted processional passageway leading to the Audience Chamber on the second floor

6 *Under an arch, a lion being subdued by a man* (perhaps Samson, or a reference to Hugh de Neville, an ancestor of Cromwell's ally Sir Thomas Neville; de Neville is said to have once torn apart a lion)

7 *A lion rampant* (Albini)

Above these roundels are seven smaller coats of arms: Bernack, Driby, Cromwell, [broken], Cromwell, Tateshale, Deyncourt. Below are seven small Treasurer's purses. The spandrels depict a rabbit eating a plant, and a dragon fighting a centaur.

FURNITURE

The two pieces of furniture are a seventeenth-century plain oak chest and a Jacobean oak refectory table.

THE SECOND FLOOR

The Audience Chamber

Leaving the south-east staircase at the second floor, one enters a long passage running almost the full length of the east wall of the tower. This served as an impressive hallway, foreshadowing the richness to come in the central chamber. It has a fine brick vault with decorative shields on the bosses. The turret room at its end has a latrine and fireplace, and perhaps served as a waiting-room for important guests.

The main room on this floor, known as the Audience Chamber, differs from the other upper rooms in that the corbels are at the far, south end, where they would probably have supported an awning under which Lord Cromwell would have sat to receive visitors who approached through the door at the north end.

CHIMNEYPIECE

The crenellated chimneypiece is decorated with ten panels of blind tracery, carved with coat of arms.

LEFT TO RIGHT:

1 *Ermine a fess* (Bernack)

2, 4, 6, 8, 10 *Treasurer's purse* (Cromwell)

3 *A fess dancetty between ten billets* (Deyncourt)

5 *Two cinquefoils, a dexter canton* (Driby)

7 *A bend and chief* (Cromwell)

9 *A chequy a chief ermine* (Tateshale)

DOVECOTE

The south-west turret room was converted around 1700 into a dovecote by inserting plaster nesting boxes.

FURNITURE

The furnishings in this room were purchased by Lord Curzon and consist of three fifteenth- and sixteenth-century oak chests and a sixteenth-century great oak table, dated 1586, with a replacement top of elm. New oak benches were inserted into the window bays during the restoration.

TAPESTRIES

The tapestries are (from left to right) *The Triumph of Alexander the Great* and *Aeneas and Achates in the presence of Queen Dido*, both seventeenth-century Flemish tapestries. The two Biblical scenes are sixteenth-century Brussels tapestries and depict *Jephthah greeted by his daughter after his victory over the Amorites* and *Isaac presenting Rebekah to Abraham*. The tapestries were purchased by Lord Curzon from Bernheimer in Munich for £1,160 in July 1913.

THE THIRD FLOOR

The Private Chamber

The small lobby to the third floor has elaborate window tracery and a complex vaulted ceiling with the intersecting ribs forming a star. Immediately to the left is the entrance to the hall. Ahead, is a small room in the east wall.

The main room on the third floor was the withdrawing or private chamber where Lord Cromwell may have slept.

CHIMNEYPIECE

The crenellated chimneypiece is decorated with eleven panels of blind tracery, decorated with coats of arms.

LEFT TO RIGHT:

1, 3, 5, 7, 9, 11 *Treasurer's purse* (Cromwell)

2 *A fess dancetty between ten billets* (Deyncourt)

4 *Two cinquefoils, a dexter canton* (Driby)

6 [blank]

8 *A bend and chief* (Cromwell)

10 *Ermine a fess* (Bernack)

In the spandrels of the fire arch there is an ingenious device – the Treasurer's purse lying on a plant that has been identified as the Common Gromwell (*Lithospermum officinale*), a native weed. The device is a rebus (ie pun on Cromwell's name). According to Gerard's *Herball* (1597), the seeds of the Common Gromwell 'driveth forth the stone'. This cure for gallstones was perhaps already appreciated in Cromwell's day.

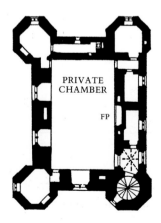

Third Floor

THE ROOF AND BATTLEMENTS

The staircase next leads on to the machicolation gallery, built on the thickness of the wall, with an open arcade facing inwards towards the roof. The galleries project outwards on corbels to create the overhang necessary for the machicolation holes through which missiles could be dropped on attackers at the base of the tower. Although rare in England, this feature was common from the thirteenth to the fifteenth centuries in France, where it would have been seen by Cromwell when he was fighting in the French wars under Henry V. Each bay is lit by a window and has two sloped apertures below. The shutters and grills are part of Lord Curzon's reconstruction.

The parapet walk round the battlements was carried on the gallery roof, which is a modern construction, as indeed is a good deal of the brickwork and coping at this level, which may explain the decorative appearance of the battlements. Four corner turrets rise above the gallery. The staircase ends in a brick vault, but a narrow staircase in the thickness of the south-east turret wall leads to its roof (not open to visitors). The other three turrets have rooms at both levels with fireplaces in the lower set; roof access was through trap doors.

From the roof the visitor has superb views of the flat surrounding countryside and of the series of wards and moats which formed the principal defences of Tattershall.

THE CHURCH

To the east of the castle stands the collegiate church of the Holy Trinity, which Cromwell willed to be built in place of a Norman chapel. His earliest surviving will of 1431 makes provision for a chantry in the parish church, ie an endowment for priests to celebrate masses for the souls of himself and his family. However, he soon extended his vision to encompass the foundation of a collegiate church served by a 'college' of priests. In 1439 he obtained a licence for it from Henry VI, who himself was to found collegiate chapels at Eton and King's College, Cambridge. In the following year a charter established the college and named its first members.

Lord Cromwell never lived to see his final project completed, but his will allowed for the sale of other properties to fund it. The financing and construc-

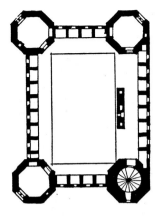

Roof Level

*(Right) An arcaded gallery
runs round the roof of the
Great Tower. The octagonal
corner turrets were originally
topped by spires, which are
visible in the engraving
illustrated on p.28. Much of
the brickwork at this level was
reconstructed by Lord Curzon*

tion of the church was overseen by Cromwell's chief executor, William Waynflete, Bishop of Winchester.

The church was built *c.*1465–85 by the architect John Cowper. It is constructed of limestone in the Perpendicular style and remains one of the largest parish churches in the county.

The Interior

Lord Cromwell and his wife are buried beneath the floor to the left of the altar but there is no indication of their graves, as the floor was repaved in the nineteenth century.

The east window in the chancel contains the fragments of stained glass that remain from the original windows. Building accounts of 1482 give details of their installation. In 1754, following complaints from the minister that he could not read his homilies in the gloom, Lord Fortescue, the church's patron, sold the stained glass to the Earl of Exeter

for his chapel at Burghley and St Martin's church, Stamford. The latter agreed to replace it with plain glass.

The Treasurer's purse can be seen in the window and also carved into the wood on the lower part of the pulpit.

The stone screen which separates the chancel from the nave was erected in 1528 by Robert de Whalley, who was a member of the college. He is buried beneath the screen.

THE NORTH TRANSEPT

This would have originally been a chapel but it now serves as a protected area for the memorial brasses. The remaining portions depict:

Ralph, Lord Cromwell (the missing portion originally showed his wife, Margaret Deyncourt)

William Moor, the second warden of the College

Sir William Symson

The fifteenth-century guardhouse (now used as a museum)
and the church

John Gygor, a priest

Lady Joan Stanhope and Maud, Lady Willoughby
d'Eresby (Cromwell's nieces and heirs)

Being the parish church of Tattershall, the building is not owned by the National Trust and for its
income it relies on the efforts of the local congrega-
tion and the generosity of visitors.

COLLEGE BUILDINGS

Excavations have revealed parts of the brick ranges
of the college courts that stood to the east and south
of the church. In 1967 the brick foundations of a
gateway were found in the outer court. It had a
doorway flanked by polygonal towers and faced
north across the large open space that since the 1790s
has been crossed by the Horncastle Canal. This area
must have resembled the great court of a monastery,
for the precinct wall extended into the village.

The ruin of another two-storeyed fifteenth-
century building contains the blocked archways of
a gateway through the precinct wall. Known as the
college building, it may have been designed to
serve as stables or offices on the ground floor with
college servants' quarters above. This building is
now in the care of Heritage Lincolnshire and may
be reached from the market square.

THE BEDEHOUSES

Cromwell's will also requested the establishment of
an almshouse to be known as the 'Cromwell Bede-
house'. Between the church and the road is a row
of seventeenth-century almshouses, presumably on
the site of their fifteenth-century predecessors.
Almshouses were actually founded in 1440, but
among the estate papers there is a note in 1486 of the
transfer of a timber-framed building from another
site to be used at Tattershall for this purpose.

(Right) The church was endowed by Ralph Cromwell and
built after his death by his executor, William Waynflete,
Bishop of Winchester

TATTERSHALL
AND ITS OWNERS

RALPH, LORD CROMWELL
(1393–1456)

'Have I not the right?'

The man who built the Great Tower of Tattershall Castle was a powerful landowner, subtle politician, and successful financier, diplomat and soldier, praised by his contemporaries for the elegance of his manners and for his 'succession of ornate phrases'. Above all, he was immensely conscious of his status and position, which he was determined to defend by every legal means possible, unlike most of the other great magnates of the mid-fifteenth century, whose increasing resort to violence was to precipitate the Wars of the Roses. Cromwell's belief in the justice of his own cause was expressed most succinctly in his defiant motto, *Nay je droit* ('Have I not the right?'). This proud self-confidence took its most enduring form in Tattershall Castle.

Ralph Cromwell was born in 1393 into a wealthy family, which had established substantial estates in the Midlands by a series of judicious marriages. His grandfather's family was descended from the Cromwells of Nottinghamshire, who had held a seat in the village of that name since the twelfth century. Tattershall itself came to Lord Cromwell's grandmother, Maud de Bernack, from the de Tatershales, who were themselves descended from Eudo, recorded as Lord of Tattershall in 1086. Heir to these estates and to his father's barony, Cromwell was already guaranteed a considerable position as a medieval lord.

Early in the 1400s, when not yet in his teens, Ralph Cromwell entered the service of the Duke of Clarence, second son of Henry IV, thanks to the influence of his uncle, William Cromwell, who had served the King before his accession. In 1415 the young Ralph fought at Agincourt under Henry V, who rapidly promoted him to command various garrisons in France and in 1420 appointed him a negotiator at the Treaty of Troyes. Later he was to be present at the trial and burning of Joan of Arc in Rouen.

After succeeding as 3rd Lord Cromwell in 1417 and inheriting most of the estate on the death of his grandmother Maud two years later, he could have retired to his Midlands domain. However, he remained in royal service where his skills as administrator and diplomat made him one of the King's most trusted advisers. He later proudly claimed to have 'spent his youghthe and goodes in such service... withoute any blemishe or defylinge of their name or worshipp'. It was natural, therefore, that when Henry V died in 1422, Cromwell should be appointed to the Council for the infant King Henry VI. The Council opposed the idea of giving the King's uncle, the Duke of Gloucester, the supreme authority of a Regent, conferring on him instead the more limited position of Protector. When Cromwell was summarily dismissed from his post as King's Chamberlain by Gloucester in 1432, he protested that the act was illegal, but to Gloucester that was irrelevant. Under a weak monarch, the rule of law was increasingly set aside, as powerful nobles of the royal blood vied for power. If a lesser courtier like Cromwell was to survive in this dangerous world, he needed allies; he looked for help particularly to Henry Beaufort, Bishop of Winchester. Land and money also offered some measure of protection, and he bolstered his position in the time-honoured family manner in 1423 by marrying the heiress Margaret Deyncourt, who brought with her further Midlands estates. He was particularly clever at exploiting every loophole in property law to increase his landed possessions.

Lord Cromwell's political career reached its climax in 1433, when he was appointed Lord Treasurer to Henry VI. He was to hold the post for the

Ralph, Lord Cromwell and his wife, Margaret Deyncourt. An engraving based on an early drawing of the memorial brass in Tattershall church, which has since been defaced

The Parlour chimneypiece is carved with Cromwell's purse of office as Lord Treasurer and his motto, 'Nay je droit' ('Have I not the right?'), interspersed with the arms of the wealthy families into which the Cromwells married

next ten years – longer than anyone else in the fifteenth century: an extraordinary achievement in this period of severe political instability. As Treasurer, he was responsible for administering the royal finances, which were suffering from the costs of the French wars. Cromwell was an active and able financier who attempted to reschedule the crown's debts and curb abuses by senior courtiers, but with little success. With this post came numerous other offices, each bringing Cromwell grants of property and associated payments. He succeeded the Duke of Bedford as Master of the Mews and Falconer to Henry VI, and in 1444 he was granted for life the positions of Constable of Nottingham Castle and Warden of Sherwood Forest.

Cromwell profited hugely from his position as Treasurer (in 1446–8 his annual income was over £2,000) and he proudly took the Treasurer's purse as his badge. But he was also conscious that in the turbulent world of the 1430s he could lose office at any moment. To buttress his position, he poured his vast income into an ambitious programme of new building on his estates at Tattershall, South Wingfield Manor in Derbyshire and Collyweston in Northamptonshire. In 1446–8 he spent no less than 4,000 marks on Tattershall Castle alone.

The Great Tower is one of the masterpieces of English medieval brickwork. The huge traceried windows on the west front suggest that it was built as much for display as defence

THE BUILDING OF THE CASTLE

Ralph Cromwell was Lord Treasurer at a time when the Crown was politically and financially weak. In this climate Cromwell's expenditure on his estates signified almost unchallengeable power. Magnificence of buildings, hospitality and costume (including household liveries) expressed wealth and encouraged support.

Tattershall Castle is one of the three most important surviving mid-fifteenth-century brick castles in England. The others are Caister Castle in Norfolk,

which was built in 1432–46 by Sir John Fastolf, a friend of Cromwell and, like him, a veteran of the French wars; and Herstmonceux Castle in Sussex, which was begun in 1441 for Sir Roger Fiennes, Treasurer of the Household to Henry VI and so a close colleague of Cromwell.

Five accounts survive for works at the castle at Tattershall between February 1434 and March 1446, which provide information on the sources of materials and the names of craftsmen. Unfortunately, however, it is extremely difficult to identify the nature of the work that is recorded. The 'great tower called le Dongeon' is not referred to until 1445–6, but if the 'parlour' mentioned in 1435 refers to its ground-floor room, then work had probably been under way on it for two or three years already. The comparable, but smaller, brick tower at Farnham in Surrey, which was put up by Cromwell's executor, William Waynflete, is known to have been built in six years, 1470–5.

In the 1430s brick was still a relatively novel building material in England. Its introduction was encouraged by migrant workmen from the brick-building areas of Flanders and northern Germany, who seem to have settled around Hull from the fourteenth century. The building accounts for Tattershall reveal that in 1434–5 'Baldwin Doche-man' (Dutchman) supervised the firing of 500,000 large 'tiles' (ie bricks) for the Great Tower, which were produced nine miles to the north at Edlington Moor and twelve miles to the south at Boston.

The architect of the tower is unknown, but John Cowper of Tattershall, master mason of the church and college, which were built c.1465–85, seems to have been strongly influenced by it. He was in charge of building Kirkby Muxloe, Leicestershire, for Lord Hastings, which retains a small gatehouse and tower of similar design with diapered brick-work.

The fifteenth-century English tower-houses like Tattershall developed from the keep of the Norman castle, although the latter had been passing out of fashion since the thirteenth century, especially in the south. While serving in the French wars, Cromwell had probably seen the high towers of the castles at Pierrefonds and Véz, which both contain well-lit principal rooms of the kind found at Tattershall. He had certainly visited the Château de Vincennes near Paris, the most impressive of all the fourteenth-century residential towers. He may have also noted the brick castles of Picardy and Flanders. Tattershall probably has no one source, but rather is a combination of influences from Cromwell and his migrant brick workers.

The debate continues as to whether the Great Tower was built for show or defence. By the 1430s most owners were building more comfortable un-fortified manor houses, and even in the less settled Scottish borders and northern England the keep was no longer considered the best solution for domestic fortification. The machicolation (missile) holes round the parapet, which were copied from French castles, could have been used in a siege, but the elegant and large ground-floor windows suggest that Cromwell did not expect to have to put them to the test. In any case, he could rely on the series of gatehouses, curtain walls and moats created for the earlier castle to repel attackers. The Great Tower seems to have been designed principally as a statement of self-confidence and authority, which would inspire respect both from his allies and his huge retinue, who were always likely to be a more reliable form of defence than fortifications.

It is significant that Cromwell's other main residence, South Wingfield Manor in Derbyshire, was built as an unfortified manor house. As the great-grandson of the heiress Amice de Bellers, Cromwell fought a legal battle with Henry de Pierrepont for South Wingfield, having to relinquish other Derbyshire and Nottinghamshire estates to secure it. Litigation ended in 1439, and after he had demolished previous buildings on the site, he began work, which continued until around 1450. Although South Wingfield Manor is now a ruin, it has been little altered since Cromwell's time, and the substantial surviving remains demonstrate that it was conceived on a palatial scale. It was laid out around two huge courtyards, and, just as at Tattershall, there were generous lodgings for his household, an audience chamber in which to receive visitors, and a set of grand apartments for Cromwell, his family and most favoured guests, arranged one above another in the High Tower.

THE TATTERSHALL HOUSEHOLD

According to Sir John Fastolf's secretary, William of Worcester, Ralph Cromwell had at least 100 people in his household at Tattershall, some of whom would have travelled with him between his various estates. A late medieval nobleman of Cromwell's status would have had a large retinue of officers, some requiring their own accommodation. These may have included a steward (estate manager), chamberlain (household), keeper of the wardrobe (materials for robes and livery) and marshall of the hall (supervising entry, keeping order and controlling access to his master). The butler, sergeant pantler and clerk of the kitchen all had their own staff.

Cromwell's large household not only provided a personal bodyguard and administered the castle and

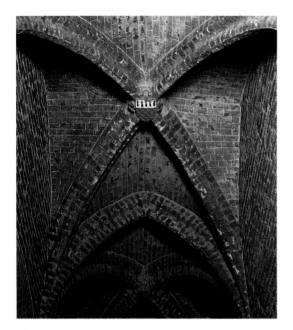

Cromwell's most honoured guests would have processed in state to the Audience Chamber on the second floor along the passageway beneath this brick vault, which is decorated with the Tateshale coat of arms

the surrounding estate, but also organised the lavish entertainment which a royal official of his importance was expected to lay on for guests. The household accounts for 1444–6 still survive, in which are recorded all the provisions bought for banquets and less grand occasions. They include 185 swans for Lord Cromwell's table at a cost of 2d each. In 1475 the inhabitants of the castle were still eating well, if the cook's accounts are any guide:

Wednesday, 19 June: paid for fresh salmon – 6d. In soles purchased – 5d. In smelts – 1d. In welks – 1d. In crabs – 7d. In the caterer's expenses at Boston – 2d.

Much of Cromwell's building work at Tattershall was designed to provide for the needs of his household and their horses. On the Middle Ward the partly exposed foundations reveal a building range which may have been lodgings. Buck's view of 1726 also shows many more buildings on the Inner Ward, which must have housed some staff. The building of lodgings to cater for increasing numbers of workers and guests was important in the development of later medieval houses and led to

the rise of the courtyard plan, which was employed at South Wingfield. A group of buildings described as 'courts' also once lay to the east of Tattershall church.

CROMWELL'S LAST YEARS

Cromwell's frenzied decade of building slowed in 1443, when he resigned as Lord Treasurer, claiming that he wanted to spend his remaining years in quiet retirement and pleading 'the grete disese of sikenesse that he hath and is lykely to have if...he sholde longer occupie the said office'. However, this may have been something of a diplomatic illness, as by the 1440s Cromwell found his political

Design for the stained-glass window with the coats of arms of Ralph, Lord Cromwell and his wife, Margaret Deyncourt, commissioned by Lord Curzon in 1918

position being gradually eroded; indeed his life was now in serious danger. Beaufort and several of his other allies were dead, and his chief enemy, the Duke of Suffolk, was becoming increasingly reckless. On the afternoon of 28 November 1449 Cromwell was about to enter a Council meeting when he was attacked by William Tailboys and a group of armed men. He escaped unharmed, and turned to Parliament to indict Suffolk. Suffolk fell from power the following year, but Cromwell had made two further powerful enemies in the Dukes of Somerset and Exeter.

Cromwell's family had risen to power through marriage, and he now used the same device to protect that power. He had no children, and so his heirs were his sister's two daughters, Maud and Joan. He made an alliance with the influential Neville family by marrying Maud to Sir Thomas Neville at Tattershall in 1453. But it was symptomatic of Cromwell's weakening position that he was obliged to make the Nevilles a loan of £1,800 as part of the marriage settlement. And as the wedding party rode north to the Neville estates in Yorkshire, it was ambushed by the Percys at the head of a band of 700 men; somehow the wedding couple survived, but the following year Cromwell felt the need for further insurance, marrying his other niece, Joan, to Humphrey Bourchier, the nephew of the Duke of York. However, he was equally anxious not to be seen openly to be taking sides in the bitter power struggle that broke out between the Yorkist and Lancastrian factions after Henry VI lapsed into insanity in 1453. Nevertheless, he was implicated in planning the attack led by the Duke of York and the Nevilles on the King and the Percys at the first Battle of St Albans on 22 May 1455, which marked the opening of the Wars of the Roses. Cromwell protested his innocence when Sir Thomas Neville's own brother, the Earl of Warwick, turned on him, declaring in front of the King that he was 'the begynner of all that journey at St Albones'. It is true that Cromwell had not joined the battle, but he had certainly been collecting additional troops to support the Yorkists. He seems finally to have concluded, after a lifetime of relying on the law, that only physical force could save him from his enemies.

Perhaps fortunately, Cromwell was spared from witnessing the gradual disintegration of the rule of law. He was spending the following Christmas at South Wingfield, when on 4 January 1456 he suddenly collapsed in his chamber. The Bishop of Chester, who was a guest, 'toke a glasse and helde afore the mouthe of the saide lorde and sume lyfe appered in the same. And after that within a while helde a glasse before the mouthe of the saide lorde and then appered no lyf but was passed than whan god had so determined.' He was 62.

To the end, Ralph, Lord Cromwell remained the master of his own destiny, and true to his motto: 'Have I not the right?' His final will of 1454 provided for the building of Tattershall College and almshouses and the rebuilding of Lambley church, Nottinghamshire, where his parents were buried. Revoking an earlier will, he largely deprived his heirs, his two nieces, of all but their rights to his entailed property – only about one-third of his huge estate. The rest was to be put up for sale by his executors, who were free to choose the bene-

William Waynflete, Bishop of Winchester, was Cromwell's executor and constructed Tattershall church in his memory; portrait in Eton College

ficiaries. One of the executors was Cromwell's friend, William Waynflete, Bishop of Winchester, who used a large proportion of the proceeds to endow Magdalen College, Oxford. Cromwell also left an endowment to pay for 3,000 masses to be said in his name. As Rhoda Friedrichs concluded in her study of Cromwell's wills: 'If Cromwell could not take his wealth with him, at least he could see that it was spent not for their [his heirs'] advantage, but for the benefit of his own soul.' In life, Cromwell built impressive earthly monuments; by his last will he tried to secure a place in the heavenly mansions.

DECLINE AND ABANDONMENT

When Cromwell's heirs discovered the terms of his will, they were, perhaps not surprisingly, furious. His nieces' husbands, Thomas Neville and Humphrey Bourchier, both attended the funeral at Tattershall and immediately afterwards began stripping the castle of whatever they could carry off. Over £2,000 worth of goods, money and provisions were removed from the castle, which was inherited by Joan Bourchier. Whether she lived here is not clear; her husband certainly preferred South Wingfield Manor, which he occupied by force in 1457. Both Neville and Bourchier were to die in the Wars of the Roses, the latter at the Battle of Barnet in 1471, when Tattershall was confiscated by the Crown. It was subsequently granted by Henry VII to his mother, Margaret Beaufort, Countess of Richmond, and in 1537 by Henry VIII to Charles Brandon, 1st Duke of Suffolk in gratitude for his part in suppressing the Lincolnshire rebellion known as the Pilgrimage of Grace, during which Tattershall was occupied by the insurgents.

Little is known about how the castle was used by Suffolk, but we can assume that it remained a grand residence. An inventory of furnishings taken on his death in 1545 includes beds, Turkey carpets and hangings. Among the hangings were some representing the months, and four pieces 'of Alexander', ie Alexander the Great. (By happy coincidence, one of the tapestries bought by Curzon to refurnish the castle represents a similar subject.) Several testers (probably for beds and to hang as a ceremonial

Design for the stained-glass window with the coats of arms of Theophilus, 4th Earl of Lincoln and his wife, Bridget Fiennes

canopy above a dais) were mentioned, including one 'of the richest purple velvet, roses and percoules', ie the Tudor rose and portcullis. Conceivably, this may have been a survival from the time when the castle was a royal possession.

In his will, Suffolk asked to be buried in Tattershall church; in the event, he was interred in St George's Chapel, Windsor, in 1545, but he left £100 to be distributed among 'the poorest Households of his Tenants and others dwelling next to his Houses of Tatshall, Gresham, Ellow and Grymsthorpe in Com. Linc. [Lincolnshire]'. After reverting to the Crown, Tattershall was recovered by Sir Henry Sidney, who sold it in 1573–4 to Edward, 9th Lord Clinton, later Earl of Lincoln. It was to remain in the possession of the Earls of Lincoln until 1693.

Tattershall provided some of the earliest European settlers in America. The 4th Earl of Lincoln and his wife had strong Puritan sympathies, and the

Countess fitted out a ship, renamed the *Arbella* after her daughter, which sailed from Southampton in 1630 for the Massachusetts Bay Colony. In it travelled Thomas Dudley, steward of the castle, his daughter Anne and her husband, Simon Bradstreet, a member of the Earl's household. Bradstreet later became Governor of the Colony and was Overseer of Harvard College for 40 years.

After Tattershall was abandoned by Francis, 6th Earl of Lincoln in 1693, it passed to the Fortescue family, who never lived in the castle. There ensued 200 years of gradual decline: the moats were filled in, the grounds became an extension of the neighbouring farm, and the tower was used as a glorified cattle shed. When Samuel Buck drew his view of the castle from the east in 1726 (illustrated on p. 6), the buildings surrounding the Great Tower were largely roofless shells. An agent of the Duke of Newcastle surveyed the manors and farm of Tattershall around 1762:

Tattershall from the west in the late eighteenth century; engraving by Stewart & Burnett after J. R. Thompson. It shows the spires that once topped the corner turrets

There are the Ruins of an Antient Castle Situate near the Church which appears to have been Surrounded with double Ditches or Motes. One entire Tower of Curious Workmanship is Still Standing Supposed to have been Built by the Lord Cromwell....

The late eighteenth century was the great period of the romantic ruin, and Tattershall attracted numerous watercolourists, who showed it in a picturesque state of decay surrounded by cattle and hayricks. The great traveller and connoisseur of ruins, Lord Torrington, visited in July 1791, and thought it 'the most perfect, the grandest piece of brick work in the kingdom':

The ditch around is yet fenced by a wall, but all the outer buildings are pull'd down; except a part of a porters lodge and an old stable. A poor family dwell in one angle; up which staircase with an excellent grooved banister, we mounted to the top; and half around the battlements, whence is an unbounded prospect: the walls are 15 feet thick; the cross beams, and the iron work of the windows are left; but what is most to be admired are 3 antique stone chimney-pieces, laden with armorial bearings of the families above mention'd; which should be *taken care of.*

The previous year the botanist and President of the Royal Society Sir Joseph Banks of nearby Revesby Abbey had commissioned detailed floor plans and elevations of the tower. In 1811 an anonymous *Topographical Account of Tattershall*, illustrated with engravings of the castle and the heraldic chimneypieces, was published in Horncastle. A sketch plan of the castle grounds in 1842, referring to the existing archaeological remains, shows that there was still interest in the castle's historical importance. In 1872 Frederick Reed presented to Earl Fortescue a fine record of the castle in his *Illustrations of Tattershall Castle, Lincolnshire, from Measured Drawings.*

RESTORATION

Lord Curzon thought the story of how Tattershall was saved so extraordinary that none would believe it who had not been involved.

In 1910 the castle was sold by the Hon. Hugh Fortescue to a speculator, who parcelled up the estate before declaring bankruptcy. The estate had

Lord Curzon at Tattershall in 1912, when, thanks to his efforts, the chimneypieces returned to the castle

been mortgaged to a bank, which sold it on to other speculators. The castle was then bought by an American syndicate. The sale and subsequent removal of the famous fireplaces in 1911 caused a public outcry and attracted Lord Curzon's interest, as he explained:

The attention of the public having been called to the sale of the Castle and to the abstraction of the mantelpieces, which were carried off by the dealers to London, and an abortive attempt to save both having been made by the National Trust for Places of Historic Interest, I was led in the past autumn to look into the question by my interest in archaeological matters, and my strong feeling against the destruction or spoilation of one of the foremost and most splendid of our national monuments.

George Nathaniel, Lord Curzon of Kedleston (1859–1925) already had considerable experience of the protection of historic monuments. As Viceroy

of India (1898–1906), he had been involved in the setting up of commissions to preserve ancient buildings such as the Taj Mahal. He was also to restore Bodiam Castle in Sussex.

Curzon confided his next move to the Vicar of Tattershall, Mr Yglesias:

When I got back to town on Friday I found that negotiations were proceeding for the acquisition of the Castle for purposes of vandalism, if not of demolition. I therefore cut the Gordian knot by buying it myself.... I tell you this in the strictest confidence, because I do not want it to be known... that I am the purchaser.... One of my reasons for preserving secrecy is that I may want to purchase some of the adjoining land; another is that I have not abandoned all hope about the fireplaces.

The purchase of the castle was completed on 27 October 1911, and Curzon then set about trying to save the missing fireplaces. He had all the ports watched so that they should not leave the country in secret. Finally, Curzon was contacted by a dealer acting as middleman for the owners of the

The heraldic stained glass in this vaulted window recess was commissioned by Curzon to commemorate the later owners of Tattershall

tion of their findings. Weir reported that the roofless Great Tower was in a sorry state:

The years of exposure had told on the tops of the walls, which were overgrown with vegetation, and the upper courses of the brick-work were considerably perished and dislodged. In a similar manner most of the coping stones of the battlemented parapets on the main roof, and the roofs of the turrets, were missing, as well as the brick-work which had supported them.

Between 1912 and 1914 the moats were excavated and the tower restored. Tracery in the lower windows had to be replaced, as did the floors of the central rooms of the upper three floors. The roof and the detail of the battlements were reconstructed as far as the existing evidence allowed.

Lord Curzon also contributed to the decoration of the castle, commissioning new stained glass from Clayton & Bell and H. G. Wright in London, which took up the heraldic theme of the fireplaces by including the coats of arms of Ralph Cromwell's successors as owners of Tattershall. Curzon also bought early furniture and tapestries in an attempt to suggest how the interiors may have looked in Cromwell's time. The castle was officially opened to the public on 8 August 1914.

The rescue and restoration of Tattershall Castle marked an important moment in the history of the preservation movement. Curzon's public-spirited action led directly to the passing of the Ancient Monuments Act (1913), which was the basis for all subsequent legislation on the subject. On his death in 1925 both Tattershall and Bodiam Castle passed to the National Trust.

Regrettably, the breaking-up of the Clinton estate has allowed twentieth-century development to encroach on the setting of the castle, distorting our view of a place, which until then had retained its majesty and mystery as a rural fenland landscape. The National Trust's recent acquisition of further land around Tattershall Castle underlines its continuing commitment to the preservation of this towering Lincolnshire landmark.

fireplaces, which were discovered in packing cases at Tilbury docks. Curzon launched an appeal, and at a cost of £5,155 the fireplaces were saved. They were returned to Tattershall in triumph on a procession of decorated wagons in May 1912.

Buying the castle and returning the chimney-pieces was only the start. Curzon masterminded the repair work, and took a close personal interest in every stage. He engaged William Weir, a disciple of William Morris and an experienced architect much used by the Society for the Preservation of Ancient Buildings, to excavate the site and restore the buildings. He also asked the eminent medieval historian Prof. Hamilton Thompson to research Tattershall's history and he set in train the publica-

OWNERS OF TATTERSHALL

Tateshale

Albini

ROBERT DE TATESHALE* (d. 1212)
holds market at Tattershall from 1201

ROBERT DE TATESHALE = Mabel de Albini*
(d. 1249) gets licence to build stone | (d. before 1243)
castle at Tattershall 1231

ROBERT DE TATESHALE (d. 1273)

Driby

Bernack

ROBERT, 1st BARON = Johanna   JOAN = Robert de
DE TATESHALE (d. 1298) | FitzRannulph   (d. 1329) | Driby* (d. 1279)

ROBERT, 2nd BARON DE TATESHALE = Eva
(1272–1303) | Tibtoft

ROBERT, 3rd BARON DE TATESHALE (d. 1305)

Vipont

JOHN DE DRIBY   Alice = Sir William   Ralph   John = Idonea de Layburne
(d. 1334)   (d. 1341) | Bernack*   Cromwell*   (d. 1335) | co-heiress of
                                          (d. 1298)   Robert de Vipont*

John de Bernack = Joan   Ralph Cromwell = Joan de la Mare
(d. 1341) | Marmion*

Ralph Cromwell = Avice de Bellers

Marmion

MAUD DE BERNACK = Ralph, 1st Baron Cromwell
(d. 1419) | (d. 1398)

John, Lord = Joan (1386–1408)   Ralph, 2nd = Joan   Elizabeth = Sir John
Deyncourt* | dau. and co-heiress of Baron Cromwell | Clifton*
(1382–1406) | Lord Grey of Rotherfield* (d. 1417)

Cromwell

Margaret = RALPH, 3rd BARON CROMWELL   Margaret = Sir Richard
Deyncourt   (1393–1456) Lord Treasurer 1433–43   Stanhope
(d. 1454)   rebuilds Tattershall 1434–45   (d. 1436)

MAUD = (2) Sir Thomas Neville   JOAN = (1) Sir Humphrey
(d. 1497)   (d. 1460 Battle of   (d. 1481)   Bourchier
             Wakefield)   Tattershall (d. 1471 Battle
        (3) Sir Gervase Clifton   forfeited to of Barnet)
             (d. 1471 Battle of   the Crown
             Tewkesbury)   c.1471

Grey

Deyncourt

Owners of Tattershall are in CAPITALS

* denotes families whose arms are represented on the Tattershall
chimneypieces

BIBLIOGRAPHY

AVERY, Tracey, 'Wealth and Power: The Furnishings of Tattershall Castle, *c.*1450–1550', *Apollo*, April 1997.

CURZON, Marquis and Tipping, H. A., *Tattershall Castle, Lincolnshire*, London, 1929.

EMERY, A., 'Ralph, Lord Cromwell's Manor at Wingfield (1439–*c.*1450): Construction, Design and Influence', *Archaeological Journal*, cxlii, 1985, pp. 276–339.

FRIEDRICHS, R. L., 'Ralph, Lord Cromwell and the Politics of Fifteenth-Century England', *Nottingham Medieval Studies*, xxxii, 1988, pp. 207–27.

FRIEDRICHS, R. L., 'The Last Wills of Ralph, Lord Cromwell', *Nottingham Medieval Studies*, xxxiv, 1990, pp. 93–112.

GOODALL, John, 'Tattershall Castle, Lincolnshire', *Country Life*, 10 October 1996, pp. 50–55.

HAMILTON THOMPSON, A., *Tattershall: The Manor, the Castle, the Church*, Lincoln, 1928.

JOHNSON, C. P. C., 'Tattershall Castle: The Saving of a National Treasure, 1911–1914', *Lincolnshire Life*, xviii (8), 1978.

MYATT-PRICE, E. M., 'Cromwell Household Accounts, 1417–1476', A. C. Littleton and B. S. Yamey, ed., *Studies in the History of Accounting*, London, 1956, pp. 99–113.

PICKWORTH, M. A., *History of Tattershall, Lincolnshire*, Lincoln, 1901.

REED, Frederick, *Illustrations of Tattershall Castle, Lincolnshire, from Measured Drawings*, 1872; reprinted 1970.

SIMPSON, W. D., 'The Building Accounts of Tattershall Castle 1434–72', *Lincoln Record Society*, lv, 1966.

THOMPSON, M. W., 'The Construction of the Manor at South Wingfield, Derbyshire', A. Detsicas, ed., *Problems in Economic and Social Archaeology*, London, 1974.

[WEIR, G.], *A Topographical Account of Tattershall*, Horncastle, 1811.

WOOD, M., *The English Mediaeval House*, London, 1965.

The chimneypieces returning to Tattershall in June 1912